Clothing

WITHDRAWN

Kate Walker

mc **Marshall Cavendish**
Benchmark
New York

Other Marshall Cavendish Offices:
Marshall Cavendish International (Asia) Private Limited, 1 New Industrial Road, Singapore 536196 • Marshall Cavendish International (Thailand) Co Ltd. 253 Asoke, 12th Flr, Sukhumvit 21 Road, Klongtoey Nua, Wattana, Bangkok 10110, Thailand • Marshall Cavendish (Malaysia) Sdn Bhd, Times Subang, Lot 46, Subang Hi-Tech Industrial Park, Batu Tiga, 40000 Shah Alam, Selangor Darul Ehsan, Malaysia

Marshall Cavendish is a trademark of Times Publishing Limited

All websites were available and accurate when this book was sent to press.

Library of Congress Cataloging-in-Publication Data

Walker, Kate.
    Clothing / Kate Walker.
    p. cm. — (Recycling)
    Includes index.
    Summary: "Discusses how clothing is made and the variety of ways to
recycle it"—Provided by publisher.
    ISBN 978-1-60870-128-5
    1. Used clothing industry—Juvenile literature. 2. Clothing and
dress—Recycling—Juvenile literature. 3. Textile
waste—Recycling—Juvenile literature. I. Title.
    HD9940.A2W35 2010
    363.72'88—dc22
                                    2009041308

First published in 2009 by
MACMILLAN EDUCATION AUSTRALIAN PTY LTD
15–19 Claremont Street, South Yarra 3141

Visit our website at www.macmillan.com.au or go directly to www.macmillanlibrary.com.au

Associated companies and representatives throughout the world.

Copyright © Kate Walker 2009

Edited by Julia Carlomagno
Text and cover design by Christine Deering
Page layout by Christine Deering
Photo research by Legend Images
Illustrations by Gaston Vanzet

Printed in the United States

Acknowledgments

The author and the publisher are grateful to the following for permission to reproduce copyright material:

Front cover photograph: Person recycling clothes courtesy of Photolibrary/Banana Stock

Photos courtesy of: AAP Image/Wildlight, 8; © SCPhotos/Alamy, 12 right; Reg Morrison/AUSCAPE, 30; Coo-ee Picture Library, 9 center, 23; Ali Al-Saadi/AFP/Getty Images, 12 center; Daniel Mihailescu/AFP/Getty Images, 21; Jose Azel/Aurora/Getty Images, 13 left; China Photos/Getty Images, 9 right; Alison Clarke/Getty Images, 12 left; Steve Shott/Getty Images, 7 right; Russell Underwood/Getty Images, 6 right; © Ralph125/iStockphoto, 5; © 2008 Jupiterimages, 3, 22; LMB Education, 29 both; © Angus McIntosh, Natural Sciences Image Library, 30; © Peter E. Smith, Natural Sciences Image Library, 14, 15, 16; Photolibrary © Neil McAllister/Alamy, 13 right; Photolibrary © superclic/Alamy, 17; Photolibrary/Banana Stock, 1, 4; Photolibrary/ Peter Bowater, 9 left; The Seven Hills School, 26, 27; © Vadym Andrushchenko/Shutterstock, 18; © Jaimie Duplass/Shutterstock, 6 left; © Boris Katsman/Shutterstock, 20; © Brad Thompson/Shutterstock, 30; © Tomasz Trojanowski/Shutterstock, 7 left; Walker Primary School, 28.

While every care has been taken to trace and acknowledge copyright, the publisher tenders their apologies for any accidental infringement where copyright has proved untraceable. Where the attempt has been unsuccessful, the publisher welcomes information that would redress the situation.

Contents

Glossary Words

When a word is printed in **bold**, you can look up its meaning in the Glossary on page 31.

What Is Recycling?

Recycling is collecting used products and making them into new products. Recycling is easy and keeps the environment clean.

Every item of clothing that is recycled saves resources and helps the environment.

Why Recycle Clothing?

Recycling clothing helps:

- save **natural resources** for future use
- reduce **pollution** in the environment
- keep waste material out of **landfills**

If more clothing was recycled, landfills such as this one could be closed.

Types of Clothing

During summer, people wear light, loose clothing to keep them cool. During winter, people wear heavy, bulky clothing to keep them warm.

People wear hats, shirts, and shorts in summer.

People wear wool hats, coats, and pants in winter.

Day and Night Clothing

During the day many people wear special clothing for work or school. At night most people wear soft, loose clothing to sleep in.

People wear shirts, skirts, dresses, or pants, and shoes during the day.

People wear pajamas, bathrobes, and slippers at night.

How Clothing Is Made

Clothing is made from **fibers**. Clothing fibers come from different natural resources.

- Cotton fibers come from cotton plants.
- Wool fibers come from sheep's wool.
- **Artificial** fibers come from plastic.

Cotton plants are collected so the fibers can be made into cloth.

The Process of Making Clothing

Fibers go through a three-stage **process** of spinning, weaving, and sewing when people make clothing.

Stage 1
Fibers are spun into thread.

Stage 2
Thread is woven into cloth.

Stage 3
Cloth is cut into different shapes. Shapes are sewn together into clothing.

Throwing Away Clothing or Recycling Clothing?

Throwing away clothing uses natural resources, increases pollution, and adds to waste.

Which Resources Are Lost When Clothing Is Thrown Away?

Natural Resources		• More water is used to grow cotton
Pollution		• More water is polluted by wool-cleaning chemicals • More harmful chemicals are released into the air when plastic is turned into artificial fibers
Waste		• More land is used for landfills

Recycling clothing saves natural resources, reduces pollution, and cuts down on waste. Which do you think is better, throwing away or recycling clothing?

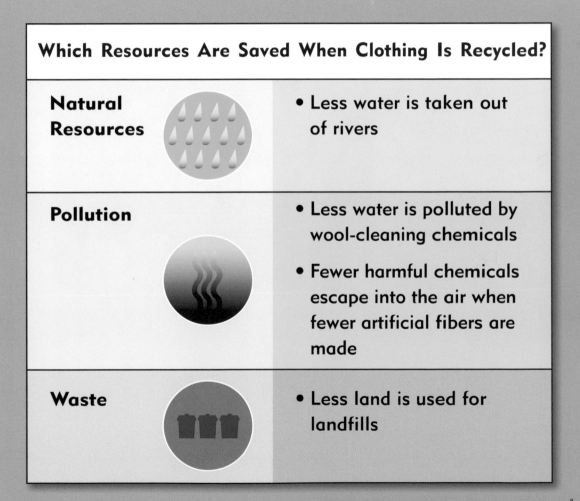

Which Resources Are Saved When Clothing Is Recycled?

Natural Resources		• Less water is taken out of rivers
Pollution		• Less water is polluted by wool-cleaning chemicals • Fewer harmful chemicals escape into the air when fewer artificial fibers are made
Waste		• Less land is used for landfills

How Clothing Is Recycled

Used clothing is collected by **textile** recyclers or **donated** to **charity organizations**. They sort the clothing into grades. Different grades of used clothing are recycled in five different ways.

1. Thrift stores
Good used clothing is sold in thrift stores to raise money for charity. It is also sold in resale shops.

2. Overseas markets
Good used clothing is shipped overseas and sold in markets.

3. Cleaning wipes
Clean cotton clothes are made into rags, which are sold to industries as cleaning wipes.

4. Stuffing material

Clean artificial-fiber clothes are sold to industries and used as stuffing material for mattresses.

5. Respun fibers

Clean wool and artificial-fiber clothes are made into rags, **shredded**, and respun into new fibers.

Recycling Clothing at Home

Used clothing can be recycled from home by donating it to a thrift store. Some charity organizations set up clothing collection bins in busy places, such as parking lots.

Clothing can be recycled by putting it in a clothing collection bin.

How to Recycle Clothing

The correct way to recycle clothing is:
- wash and fold clothing
- keep matching garments together
- put clothing into a clean bag and tie it closed

Keep matching garments together when recycling clothing.

Can All Clothing Be Recycled?

Not all clothing can be recycled. Clothing that is very dirty is **nonrecyclable**. Clean, torn clothing is recycled to make cleaning wipes, stuffing material, or new fibers.

Very dirty or stained clothing should go in the garbage can.

Clothing made from other types of material, such as leather, can also be recycled. Household goods made of woven fiber, such as sheets, are also recyclable.

Other Clothing and Household Goods that Can Be Recycled

Other recyclable clothing	Other recyclable woven-fiber products
✓ shoes	✓ sheets
✓ bags and purses	✓ blankets
✓ belts	✓ curtains
✓ leather jackets	✓ towels
✓ plastic raincoats	✓ stuffed toys

Is Recycling Clothing the Best Option?

Recycling clothing saves water and stops air pollution. However, recycling clothing also uses resources. Trucks and ships that transport recycled clothing burn **fossil fuels**.

Ships that take clothing overseas burn fossil fuels in their engines.

Machines that shred used clothing to make new fibers use **electricity**. Machines that spin recycled fiber or cut and sew recycled cloth also use electricity.

All machines that turn old clothing into new clothing use electricity.

Reducing and Reusing Clothing

There are many ways to reuse clothing or to reduce the amount of clothing we use. One way is to take care of the clothing we have.

Wearing an old shirt over good clothing protects it from paint spatters.

Some simple ways to reuse clothing or reduce the amount of clothing we use are:

- change into old clothing when doing dirty jobs
- buy clothing only when it is needed
- shop for **secondhand** clothing in resale shops

Clothing lasts longer when hung up in a closet.

Make a Hand Puppet

Scraps of cloth or damaged clothing can be useful. Make a lively puppet from a square of cloth.

What You Will Need:
- a square of cloth about 12 inches x 12 inches (30 cm x 30 cm)
- four cotton balls
- a rubber band
- felt-tip markers
- scissors
- glue
- scraps of cloth

What to Do:

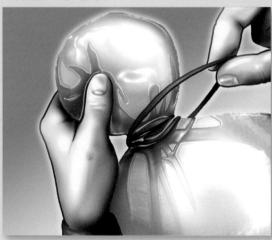

1. Place the cotton balls in the center of the cloth. Bring the corners of the cloth together and tie the rubber band just below the cotton balls.

2. Poke your middle finger through the neck and stretch out your thumb and pinkie finger. Mark the cloth above your pinkie finger and thumb.

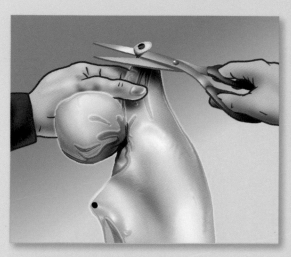

3. Remove the puppet from your hand and cut two holes where you made the dots.

4. Put your fingers through these holes to make your puppet's arms. Draw a face and decorate the body with scraps of cloth.

School Recycling Projects

Seven Hills School in Cincinnati, Ohio, does more than collect used clothing for recycling. It has even set up its own resale shop.

The Resale Shop at Seven Hills School is run by staff, as well as parent and student volunteers.

All goods sold in the shop are donated by members of the school community. The money raised is used to fund student programs.

The Resale Shop began fifty years ago and today sells used clothing, furniture, and books.

Recycling Clothing and Shoes

Walker Primary School in the United Kingdom has a giant clothing recycling bin at the front gate. Students put used clothing into the bin for recycling.

Walker Primary School's giant clothing recycling bin is called Berty Bank.

Inside the school is another bin for collecting pairs of used shoes. Walker Primary School collects more than forty large bags of used shoes each year.

Students collect clothes and shoes for their local recycling company.

How Recycling Clothing Helps Animals

Growing fibers for clothing uses water. Using water from rivers destroys animal **habitats**. When you recycle clothing you save the habitats of many animals, including:

- frogs

- fish

- otters

Glossary

artificial   Made by humans.

charity organizations   Groups of people working to help those in need.

donated   Given away as a gift.

electricity   A type of power often used to run machines.

fibers   Very tiny fine threads.

fossil fuels   Oil-based fuels that power engines in cars and trucks.

habitats   Areas where animals live, feed, and breed.

landfills   Large holes in the ground where garbage is buried.

natural resources   Materials found in nature that people use and value.

nonrecyclable   Not able to be recycled.

pollution   Waste that damages the air, water, or land.

process   A series of actions that brings about a change.

secondhand   Used before by another person.

shredded   Torn into tiny pieces.

textile   Woven or knit cloth.

Index